Masterbuilt Smoker Cookbook

Top Electric Smoker Recipes for Easy and Tasty BBQ Smoking

By: Al Russler

MASTERBUILT SMOKER COOKBOOK

Legal notice

This book is copyright (c) 2017 by Al Russler. All rights are reserved. This book may not be duplicated or copied, either in whole or in part, via any means including any electronic form of duplication such as recording or transcription. The contents of this book may not be transmitted, stored in any retrieval system, or copied in any other manner regardless of whether use is public or private without express prior permission of the publisher.

This book provides information only. The author does not offer any specific advice, including medical advice, nor does the author suggest the reader or any other person engage in any particular course of conduct in any specific situation. This book is not intended to be used as a substitute for any professional advice, medical or of any other variety. The reader accepts sole responsibility for how he or she uses the information contained in this book. Under no circumstances will the publisher or the author be held liable for damages of any kind arising either directly or indirectly from any information contained in this book.

MASTERBUILT SMOKER COOKBOOK

Table of Contents

INTRODUCTION 8

PORK RECIPES 10

1-Easy Smoked Pork Butt 10

2-Smoked Pork Tenderloin 12

3-Delicious Smoked Pork Belly 14

4-Tasty Pork Shoulder 16

5-Smoked Pork Tenderloin with Honey Glazed 18

6-Smoke Pork Ribs 20

7-Perfect Pork Ribs 22

8-Spicy Smoked Pork Ribs 24

9-Yummy Smoked Pork Sliders 26

10-Smoky Pulled Pork 28

11-Honey Butter Smoked Ribs 30

12-Smoked Pork Cheese Bites 32

13-Delicious Smoked Boston Butt 34

14-Simple Smoked Pork Tenderloin 36

15-Moist Pulled Pork 38

BEEF RECIPES 40

16-Easy Beef Jerky 40

17-Smoked Beef Ribs 42

18-Simple Beef Roast 44

19-Sirloin Tip Roast 46

20-Herb Smoked Prime Rib 48

21-Smoked Short Ribs 50

22-BBQ Smoked Short Ribs 52

23-Smoked Orange Jerky 54

24-Smoked Soy Garlic Beef Jerky 56

25-BBQ thyme Smoked Brisket 58

26-Smoke Corned Beef 60

27-Smoked Beef Patties 62

28-Smoked Meatloaf 64

29-Meat Wrapped Jalapeno Peppers 66

30-Smoked Meatballs 68

POULTRY RECIPES 70

31-Smoke Whole Chicken 70

32-Smoky Wrap Chicken Breasts 72

33-Smoked Chipotle Chicken Wings 74

34-Delicious Smoked Pulled Chicken 76

35-Smoked Chicken Thighs 78

36-Simple Turkey Breast 80

37-Tasty Smoked Chicken Tenders 82

38-Cajun Seasoned Chicken Breast 84

39-Orange Smoked Chicken 86

40-Smoked Soy Chicken Legs 88

41-Delicious Honey Smoked Chicken 90

42-Smoked Buffalo Chicken Wings 92

43-Moist Wrapped Chicken Tenders 94

44-Sweet and Spicy Chicken Wings 96

45-Simple Smoked Chicken Wings 98

SEAFOOD RECIPES 100

46-Smoked Cajun Seasoned Shrimp 100

47-Simple Smoke Trout 102

48-Smoked Fish Nuggets 104

49-Smoked Orange Sesame Salmon 106

50-Smoked Wrapped Scallops 108

51-Easy Smoked Tuna 110

52-Delicious Smoked Shrimp 112

53-Smoked Dill Salmon 114

54-Easy BBQ Shrimp 116

55-Maple Peppercorns Smoked Salmon 118

56-Simple Smoked Lobster Tails 120

57-Smoked Lemon Dill Salmon 122

58-Stuffed Salmon 124

59-Delicious Sweet Salmon 126

60-Fresh and Simple Smoked Albacore Tuna 128

MASTERBUILT SMOKER COOKBOOK

INTRODUCTION

❖ What is smoking?

Smoking meat means more than just smothering it with some BBQ sauce or rubbing some smoked rub onto the meat. It is all about learning to cook your meat at the perfect temperature for the right amount of time to give it a natural smoky flavor that you would not be able to resist. Unlike many types of cooking, smoking meat is not an exact science. Smoking meat is more of an acquired skill and it is one that any person can learn. Smoking is the best way to make delicious meat dishes without working too hard at it. Smoking meat can take several hours to accomplish depending on the recipe. It can take anywhere from 1 to 12 hours to properly smoke your food, but in the end, you will be left a juicy and tender meat dish that the whole family will love.

❖ How do you smoke meat correctly?

- First apply a wet or dry rub to the meat, then place meat in zip lock bag and place in refrigerator overnight.
- Preheat the electric smoker. When the smoker is hot, add food and then a handful of wood chips the chip loading area and adjust the amount of smoke according to the recipe.
- If you are using a wet rub then pat dry meat with paper towels before putting it in the smoker.
- Maintain smoker temperature. Adjusting the damper not only changes the amount of smoke but can help regulate the temperature. Wood chips can be added as suggested for whatever you are cooking but keep the door closed as much of the time as possible so that heat does not escape.
- During final 1-2 hours, you can baste your meat with sauce or apple BBQ sauce every 30 minutes.
- Use a thermometer to determine when your meat is cooked to the proper temperature. Once it reaches the proper temperature, remove the meat from the smoker and allow to rest for 15 minutes.

❖ Types of smoking wood

- **Walnut:** This is a heavy flavor that lends itself to beef more so than pork or poultry. Walnut can be bitter if used alone and is best used with some fruit wood.

- **Cherry**: Cherry wood creates a sweet tasting smoke flavor that is great with pork and poultry. Cherry wood also lends a great color to pork butt or pork shoulder.
- **Peach:** Think of this fruit wood as milder venison of hickory great with white and pink meats.
- **Apple**: Mild, fruit flavor, perhaps the most common of the fruit woods, apple lends itself well to pork and chicken.
- **Hickory**: Hickory is a popular wood that lends hints of bacon flavor to the food you are cooking goes well with ham, beef, and pork.
- **Alder:** Alder is a mild wood from the Pacific Northwest that is good to use with seafood, pork, poultry, seafood, and light meat game.

❖ **What sauces and spice rubs are good to use when smoking meat?**
- **Dry rub ingredients:**

A dry rub is a spice mixture that is rubbed into the meat before cooking. These mixtures can be as varied as individual tastes but a basic BBQ pantry will include the following ingredients for spice rub: Thyme, salt, sage, paprika, onion powder, garlic powder, dry mustard, cumin, chili powder, black pepper.

- **Sauce Ingredients:**

The sauce combinations are endless but in general they have three main components: a fat, something sweet and something acidic. Feuds have been started over the best type of BBQ sauce with some die-hards swearing that sweet red sauce is the only sauce worthy of the name, while in other parts of the country a peppery, vinegar-heavy recipe is the sauce of choice. Regardless of the recipe and your preference, here is what you need for all your basic BBQ sauce needs: olive oil, molasses, liquid pepper sauce, lime juice, lemon juice, ketchup, hoisin sauce, coconut oil, chili sauce, brown sugar, balsamic vinegar, Worcestershire sauce, tomato paste, soy sauce, sesame oil, red wine vinegar, orange juice.

PORK RECIPES

1-Easy Smoked Pork Butt

Total Time: 16 hours 10 minutes

Serves: 12

Ingredients:

- 5 lbs bone in pork butt, trim fat to 1/4" thickness
- 1 cup apple juice
- 1/4 cup BBQ dry rub
- Wood chips, pre smoked for half hour before use

Directions:

- Preheat the smoker to 220 F/104 C.
- Season pork butt with BBQ rub and place into the smoker.
- Add two handful wood chips into the electric smoker cup.
- Smoke the meat for 16 hours.

- Spray apple juice over meat every 2 hours.
- Cook pork until internal temperature reaches 185 F/85 C.
- Chop pork and serve.

Nutritional Value (Amount per Serving):

- Calories 361
- Fat 23.4 g
- Carbohydrates 2.3 g
- Sugar 2 g
- Protein 33.5 g
- Cholesterol 117 mg

2-Smoked Pork Tenderloin

Total Time: 3 hours 10 minutes

Serves: 2

Ingredients:
- 1 pork tenderloin, trim pork tenderloin fat
- 1/4 cup BBQ sauce
- 3 tbsp dry rub

Directions:
- Preheat the smoker to 225 F/107 C.
- Rub spice mix over the pork tenderloin.
- Place meat in the smoker and smoke until internal temperature reaches at 145 F/62 C about 3 hours.
- Brush BBQ sauce over the pork when is about half hour is left to go in the smoker.

- Serve and enjoy.

Nutritional Value (Amount per Serving):

- Calories 405
- Fat 8.1 g
- Carbohydrates 15.8 g
- Sugar 8.1 g
- Protein 59.4 g
- Cholesterol 166 mg

3-Delicious Smoked Pork Belly

Total Time: 5 hours 10 minutes

Serves: 10

Ingredients:
- 5 lbs pork belly, cut into cubes and trim excess fat
- 1 cup dry rub
- 3 tbsp olive oil
- For sauce:
- 2 tbsp honey
- 3 tbsp butter
- 1 cup BBQ sauce

Directions:
- Preheat the smoker to 250 F/121 C.
- Add pork cubes, dry rub, and olive oil into the bowl and mix well.
- Place pork cubes into the smoker and smoke uncover for 3 hours.

- Remove pork cubes from smoker and place on foil pan.
- Add honey, butter and BBQ sauce and stir well.
- Cover pan with foil and place back into the smoker.
- Cook pork for another 90 minutes.
- After 90 minutes remove the foil.
- Close the lid to the smoker and smoke for 15 minutes or until sauce thickens.
- Serve and enjoy.

Nutritional Value (Amount per Serving):

- Calories 1164
- Fat 68.8 g
- Carbohydrates 12.5 g
- Sugar 10 g
- Protein 104.7 g
- Cholesterol 271 mg

4-Tasty Pork Shoulder

Total Time: 13 minutes

Serves: 12

Ingredients:
- 8 lb pork shoulder
- For rub:
- 1 tsp dry mustard
- 1 tsp black pepper
- 1 tsp cumin
- 1 tsp cayenne pepper
- 1 tsp oregano
- 1/3 cup kosher salt
- 1/4 cup garlic powder
- 1/2 cup paprika

- 1/3 cup brown sugar
- 2/3 cup sugar

Directions:

- Brine pork for 18 hours.
- Pull pork from brine and set aside for 1 hour.
- Rub mustard all over the meat.
- Combine together all rub ingredients and rub over the meat.
- Wrap meat and leave for overnight.
- Smoke meat at 250 F/121 C for 6 hours.
- Pull pork from grill and wrap in foil.
- Return pork to grill and cook for another 6 hours at 195 F/90 C.
- Shred and serve.

Nutritional Value (Amount per Serving):

- Calories 965
- Fat 65.4 g
- Carbohydrates 19.9 g
- Sugar 16.2 g
- Protein 71.6 g
- Cholesterol 272 mg

5-Smoked Pork Tenderloin with Honey Glazed

Total Time: 5 hours 10 minutes

Serves: 6

Ingredients:
- 3 lbs pork tenderloin
- 1 tsp ground cinnamon
- 1/2 cup brown sugar
- 1/4 cup honey

Directions:
- Add cinnamon, brown sugar and honey in microwave safe bowl and mix well.
- Place bowl in microwave and microwave for 15 seconds.
- Spread cinnamon mixture all over pork tenderloin.
- Place pork in the smoker and smoke at 250 F/121 C.

- After one-hour flip pork and smoke continue for 4 hours to 165 F/73 C.
- Serve and enjoy.

Nutritional Value (Amount per Serving):

- Calories 414
- Fat 8 g
- Carbohydrates 23.8 g
- Sugar 23.3 g
- Protein 59.4 g
- Cholesterol 166 mg

6-Smoke Pork Ribs

Total Time: 3 hours 10 minutes

Serves: 8

Ingredients:
- 4 lbs pork ribs
- 1/2 Tsp garlic powder
- 1/2 Tsp onion powder
- 1 tsp black pepper
- 1 tsp salt
- For sauce:
- 1/4 cup brown sugar
- 1/2 cup steak sauce
- 3/4 cup apple jelly
- 1 cup ketchup

Directions:

- Preheat the smoker to 250 F/121 C.
- In a bowl, combine together garlic powder, onion powder, pepper, and salt.
- Rub bowl mixture over the pork ribs.
- Place pork ribs on the middle rack of smoker and smoke for one hour.
- Add all sauce ingredients into the saucepan and heat over the medium heat.
- Remove pork ribs from smoker and coat with sauce.
- Wrap ribs in the foil and place into the smoker.
- Smoke ribs for another 2 hours or until tender.
- Remove ribs from smoker and coat with more sauce and serve.

Nutritional Value (Amount per Serving):

- Calories 770
- Fat 40.3 g
- Carbohydrates 37.5 g
- Sugar 28.7 g
- Protein 61.1 g
- Cholesterol 234 mg

7-Perfect Pork Ribs

Total Time: 5 hours 10 minutes

Serves: 4

Ingredients:

- 2 lbs spare rib racks
- 1/2 Tsp dried oregano
- 1/2 Tsp celery seed
- 1 tsp dry mustard
- 2 tsp cayenne
- 2 tsp salt
- 2 tsp cumin
- 1 tbsp garlic powder
- 1 tbsp black pepper
- 1/2 cup brown sugar

- 1/4 cup sweet paprika

Directions:

- Combine together all spice ingredients and rub over ribs and place in refrigerator for overnight.
- Place marinated ribs into the smoker and smoke at 220 F/104 C for 5 hours.
- Turn rib after every hour.
- Serve and enjoy.

Nutritional Value (Amount per Serving):

- Calories 667
- Fat 48.2 g
- Carbohydrates 25.3 g
- Sugar 18.9 g
- Protein 36.5 g
- Cholesterol 162 mg

8-Spicy Smoked Pork Ribs

Total Time: 4 hours 10 minutes

Serves: 8

Ingredients:
- 4 lbs pork
- 2 tsp onion powder
- 2 tsp garlic powder
- 2 tsp black pepper
- 2 tsp cayenne pepper
- 1 1/2 tbsp ground cumin
- 2 1/2 Tsp chili powder
- 1/4 cup brown sugar
- 1/2 tbsp salt
- Hickory wood chips

Directions:

- In a bowl, combine together all ingredients except pork.
- Rub spice mixture over the meat and set aside for 2 hours.
- Place pork in the smoker and cook for 3 hours at 225 F/107 C using hickory wood chips for the first two hours.
- After three hours remove pork from smoker and wrap in foil.
- Place again in the smoker and cook for another 1 hour.
- Serve and enjoy.

Nutritional Value (Amount per Serving):

- Calories 355
- Fat 8.5 g
- Carbohydrates 7 g
- Sugar 4.9 g
- Protein 60 g
- Cholesterol 166 mg

9-Yummy Smoked Pork Sliders

Total Time: 10 hours 40 minutes

Serves: 16

Ingredients:
- 8 lbs pork butt
- 1 tsp garlic pepper
- 1 tsp onion powder
- 1 tsp garlic powder
- 2 tbsp fresh lemon juice
- 1/4 cup apple cider vinegar
- 2 cups ketchup
- 16 slider rolls, split and toasted
- 6 tbsp yellow mustard
- 4 tbsp dry rub

Directions:

- Add garlic pepper, onion, powder, garlic powder, lemon juice, vinegar, and ketchup into the saucepan and simmer for 10 minutes.
- Season pork butt with a dry rub and spread mustard over the pork evenly.
- Place pork into the zip lock bag and place in refrigerator for overnight.
- Preheat the smoker to 225 F/107 C.
- Place marinated pork on middle rack of smoker and smoke for 8 hours.
- Remove pork from smoker and wrap in foil.
- Now set smoker temperature to 275 F/135 C and return pork into the smoker and smoke for another 2 hours.
- Set pork aside for half hours then pull pork and add to the slider and serve.

Nutritional Value (Amount per Serving):

- Calories 573
- Fat 16.5 g
- Carbohydrates 28.2 g
- Sugar 9 g
- Protein 74.5 g
- Cholesterol 209 mg

10-Smoky Pulled Pork

Total Time: 12 hours 10 minutes

Serves: 8

Ingredients:
- 5 lbs pork shoulder
- For brine:
- 12 oz salt
- 8 cups water
- 3/4 cup molasses
- For sauce:
- 1 tsp onion powder
- 1 tsp coriander
- 1 tsp paprika
- 1 tsp chili powder
- 1 tsp cumin
- 1 tsp fennel

Directions:
- Brine pork for 8 hours. Make sure pork is completely submerged.
- Using paper towel dry the meat.
- Combine together all rub ingredients and rub over the meat.
- Place meat in smoker and smoker for 12 hours at 200 F/93 C.
- Serve and enjoy.

Nutritional Value (Amount per Serving):
- Calories 921
- Fat 60.8 g
- Carbohydrates 23.7 g
- Sugar 17.2 g
- Protein 66.2 g
- Cholesterol 255 mg

11-Honey Butter Smoked Ribs

Total Time: 6 hours 30 minutes

Serves: 4

Ingredients:
- 1 rack pork ribs
- 1 cup BBQ sauce
- 1 cup honey
- 1 cup brown sugar
- 1/2 cup butter, sliced
- 1/4 cup apple juice
- 1 cup dry rub
- 2 tbsp olive oil

Directions:
- Coat meat with olive oil from both the sides.
- Coat meat with a dry rub from all the sides and place in refrigerator for overnight.

- Preheat the smoker and set the temperature to 225 F/107 C.
- Place meat in smoker and spritz with apple juice after every 2 hours.
- After 3 hours remove ribs from the smoker.
- Coat ribs with honey, brown sugar, and butter.
- Wrap ribs in foil and place in smoker and smoker for 2 hours.
- Remove foil and grill for 1 hour.
- Coat with BBQ sauce with 15 minutes remaining.
- Remove from smoker and serve warm.

Nutritional Value (Amount per Serving):

- Calories 805
- Fat 32.7 g
- Carbohydrates 129.8 g
- Sugar 122.6 g
- Protein 6.1 g
- Cholesterol 77 mg

12-Smoked Pork Cheese Bites

Total Time: 2 hours 45 minutes

Serves: 12

Ingredients:
- 1 egg
- 2 lbs ground pork
- 3/4 cup cheddar cheese, cut into half inch cubes
- 3 jalapeno peppers, cored and minced
- 1/3 cup BBQ sauce
- 1/3 cup milk
- 1 cup breadcrumbs
- 2 tbsp Creole seasoning

Directions:
- Set smoker to 250 F/121 C.

- In a bowl, combine together all ingredients except cheese.
- Make small ball from meat mixture and stuff cheese cubes into the each meatball.
- Place meatballs on the smoking rack and smoke until internal temperature reaches 160 F/71 C about 2 1/2 hours.
- Serve and enjoy.

Nutritional Value (Amount per Serving):

- Calories 193
- Fat 6 g
- Carbohydrates 9.7 g
- Sugar 2.9 g
- Protein 23.5 g
- Cholesterol 77 mg

13-Delicious Smoked Boston Butt

Total Time: 5 hours 10 minutes

Serves: 6

Ingredients:
- 4 lb Boston butt
- 1/4 cup apple juice
- 1 stick butter, melted
- For rub:
- 1 tbsp dry mustard
- 2 tbsp cumin
- 2 tbsp garlic powder
- 1 tsp cayenne pepper
- 1/4 cup chili powder
- 1/4 cup brown sugar
- 2 tbsp kosher salt

- 1/4 cup smoked paprika

Directions:

- Combine together all rub ingredients and rub over pork and place in refrigerator for overnight.
- Prepare smoker with hickory wood chips and charcoal.
- Smoker heat should be about 250 F/121 C.
- Place pork in the smoker and smoke for 1 hour per lb or until internal temperature reaches 190 F/87 C.
- Every hour open smoker and flip meat.
- Mop meat with apple juice and melted butter to keep it moist.
- Serve and enjoy.

Nutritional Value (Amount per Serving):

- Calories 1001
- Fat 68 g
- Carbohydrates 16 g
- Sugar 8.6 g
- Protein 80.1 g
- Cholesterol 328 mg

14-Simple Smoked Pork Tenderloin

Total Time: 3 hours 10 minutes

Serves: 4

Ingredients:

- 2 lbs pork tenderloins, cut sliver membrane
- 1/2 cup BBQ sauce
- 1/2 cup Stubb's pork marinade

Directions:

- Spread marinade over pork and place in refrigerator for overnight.
- Drain marinade and place pork into the smoker.
- Smoke pork about 3 hours at 225 F/107 C.
- About half hour before removing from smoker baste with BBQ sauce.
- When the internal temperature of pork reaches at 160 F/41 C then remove pork from smoker and wrap in foil for 10 minutes.
- Slice pork and serve.

Nutritional Value (Amount per Serving):

- Calories 505
- Fat 18.5 g
- Carbohydrates 11.8 g
- Sugar 8.6 g
- Protein 67.7 g
- Cholesterol 213 mg

15-Moist Pulled Pork

Total Time: 8 hours 10 minutes

Serves: 20

Ingredients:
- 8 lbs pork shoulder roast
- 4 cups apple cider
- For rub:
- 1 onion, chopped
- 1 tbsp garlic powder
- 1 tbsp ground black pepper
- 1 tbsp onion powder
- 2 tbsp paprika
- 2 tbsp kosher salt
- 5 tbsp brown sugar
- 5 tbsp white sugar

- 3 cups hickory wood chips

Directions:

- Place the pork shoulder into the large bowl.
- Add apple cider, garlic, powder, black pepper, onion powder, paprika, salt, brown sugar, and white sugar into the bowl.
- Cover bowl and place in refrigerator for overnight.
- Prepare smoker to 210 F/98 C.
- Add hickory wood chips into the smoker.
- Place marinated pork into the smoker and smoke for 8 hours or until tender.
- Using fork shred the pork and serves.

Nutritional Value (Amount per Serving):

- Calories 516
- Fat 37.1 g
- Carbohydrates 12.7 g
- Sugar 11.1 g
- Protein 30.9 g
- Cholesterol 128 mg

BEEF RECIPES

16-Easy Beef Jerky

Total Time: 5 hours 10 minutes

Serves: 20

Ingredients:
- 2 lbs eye round roast, cut the meat thinly
- 1 tsp red pepper flakes
- 1 tsp liquid smoke
- 2 tsp ground black pepper
- 1 tbsp honey
- 2 tbsp onion dip mix
- 2/3 cup apple cider
- 1/3 cup soy sauce
- 1/4 cup Worcestershire sauce

Directions:

- Add all ingredients into the zip lock bag expect meat and mix well.
- Add meat into the bag and massage well.
- Place meat into the refrigerator for overnight.
- Preheat the smoker to 165 F/63 C using apple wood.
- Remove meat from marinade and dry with paper towel.
- Place meat in the smoker and smoke for 5 hours.
- Serve and enjoy.

Nutritional Value (Amount per Serving):

- Calories 75
- Fat 1.7 g
- Carbohydrates 3 g
- Sugar 2.4 g
- Protein 10.7 g
- Cholesterol 20 mg

17-Smoked Beef Ribs

Total Time: 5 hours 15 minutes

Serves: 4

Ingredients:
- 2 1/2 lbs beef short ribs, trim excess fat
- 4 tbsp beef rub
- 4 tbsp olive oil
- For spritz:
- 1 cup apple juice
- 1 cup apple cider vinegar

Directions:
- Preheat the smoker to 225 F/107 C.
- Place beef in the smoker and smoke for 3 hours.
- After 1-hour spray meat after every 15 minutes. Spritz meat until wrap.

- Wrap meat in foil for 2 hours.
- Serve when meat is tender.

Nutritional Value (Amount per Serving):

- Calories 742
- Fat 39.6 g
- Carbohydrates 19.6 g
- Sugar 6.2 g
- Protein 81.9 g
- Cholesterol 258 mg

18-Simple Beef Roast

Total Time: 1 hour 5 minutes

Serves: 6

Ingredients:
- 2 lbs beef roast
- 1 tbsp ground black pepper
- 1 tbsp salt
- 1 tbsp olive oil

Directions:
- Preheat the smoker to 225 F/107 C.
- Coat beef roast with olive oil and season with pepper and salt.
- Place in smoker for 60 minutes or until internal temperature reaches 130 F/54 C.
- Wrap meat in foil and set aside for 30 minutes.
- Cut into strips and serve.

Nutritional Value (Amount per Serving):

- Calories 304
- Fat 11.8 g
- Carbohydrates 0.7 g
- Sugar 0 g
- Protein 46 g
- Cholesterol 135 mg

19-Sirloin Tip Roast

...urs 10 minutes

Ingredients:
- 2 lbs sirloin tip roast
- For marinade:
- 1/2 Tsp black pepper
- 1 tsp chili powder
- 1 tbsp onion, minced
- 1 tsp garlic, minced
- 1/2 cup brown sugar
- 1/2 cup soy sauce
- 1/2 cup Worcestershire sauce
- 1 tsp salt

Directions:

- Add roast into the zip lock bag.
- Combine together all marinade ingredients and pour into the zip lock bag.
- Seal bag and place in refrigerator for 3 hours.
- Preheat the smoker at 250 F/121 C.
- Place marinated roast into the smoker and cook for 4 hours or until internal temperature reaches 155 F/68 C.
- Serve and enjoy.

Nutritional Value (Amount per Serving):

- Calories 422
- Fat 18.1 g
- Carbohydrates 18.2 g
- Sugar 16.2 g
- Protein 42.9 g
- Cholesterol 126 mg

20-Herb Smoked Prime Rib

Total Time: 4 hours 10 minutes

Serves: 8

Ingredients:
- 5 lbs prime rib, trim excess fat
- 2 tbsp ground black pepper
- 1/4 cup olive oil
- 2 tbsp kosher salt
- For herb paste:
- 1/4 cup olive oil
- 1 tbsp fresh sage
- 1 tbsp fresh thyme
- 1 tbsp fresh rosemary
- 3 garlic cloves

Directions:

- Add all herb ingredients into the blender and blend until combined.
- Preheat the smoker to 225 F/ 107 C.
- Coat rib with olive oil and season with pepper and salt.
- Place season rib roast into the smoker and cook for 4 hours.
- Remove rib from smoker and set aside for 30 minutes.
- Cut into the slices and serve.

Nutritional Value (Amount per Serving):

- Calories 936
- Fat 81.4 g
- Carbohydrates 2 g
- Sugar 0 g
- Protein 46.9 g
- Cholesterol 204 mg

21-Smoked Short Ribs

Total Time: 4 hours 10 minutes

Serves: 6

Ingredients:
- 3 lbs short ribs, trimmed
- 1/2 cup dry rub
- 1/4 cup olive oil
- 1/2 cup ground black pepper
- 1/2 cup kosher salt
- For spritz:
- 1/3 cup Worcestershire sauce
- 1/3 cup dry red wine
- 1/3 cup beef broth
- For braising:
- 2 tbsp butter
- 1 tbsp rub

- 1 cup beef broth
- 1 cup dry red wine

Directions:

- Preheat the smoker to 225 F/107 C with wood chips.
- Season meat with black pepper and salt.
- Place seasoned ribs into the smoker for 2 hours.
- After 2 hours spritz ribs after every 30 minutes for 2 hours.
- Combine together all braising ingredients into the aluminum pan.
- Add ribs to the aluminum pan and cover the pan with foil.
- Place pan in the smoker and cook for about 2 hours.
- Once internal temperature reaches 205 F/96 C then removes meat from smoker and set aside for 15 minutes.
- Remove ribs from pan and serve.

Nutritional Value (Amount per Serving):

- Calories 1060
- Fat 94.7 g
- Carbohydrates 6.4 g
- Sugar 3.1 g
- Protein 33.3 g
- Cholesterol 181 mg

22-BBQ Smoked Short Ribs

Total Time: 5 hours 10 minutes

Serves: 4

Ingredients:
- 2 1/2 lbs beef short ribs
- 4 tbsp beef rub
- 4 tbsp olive oil
- For spritz:
- 1 cup apple juice
- 1 cup apple cider vinegar
- For bath:
- 2 tbsp Worcestershire sauce
- 2 tbsp dry rub
- 2 tbsp butter
- 1 cup beef broth

- 1 cup red wine

Directions:

- Preheat the smoker to 225 F/107 C.
- Coat ribs with beef rub and olive oil.
- Place ribs in the smoker for 3 hours.
- After 1-hour start spritz. Spritz meat after every 15 minutes.
- Add all bath ingredients into the aluminum pan then place ribs in pan and cover with foil.
- Place pan in the smoker for 2 hours or until internal temperature of the meat reaches 200 F/93 C.
- Remove ribs from bath and serve.

Nutritional Value (Amount per Serving):

- Calories 859
- Fat 45.7 g
- Carbohydrates 10.9 g
- Sugar 8.4 g
- Protein 83.2 g
- Cholesterol 273 mg

23-Smoked Orange Jerky

Total Time: 4 hours 10 minutes

Serves: 4

Ingredients:

- 1 1/2 lbs lean beef, sliced 1/4 inch slices
- 1 orange zest
- 3/4 Tsp salt
- 1 cup orange juice
- 1/2 cup orange beef sauce

Directions:

- Add all ingredients into the zip lock bag and mix well.
- Place zip lock bag in the refrigerator for overnight.
- Preheat the smoker to 170 F/76 C.
- Drain meat well and place in smoker and smoke for 4 hours.

- Serve and enjoy.

Nutritional Value (Amount per Serving):

- Calories 346
- Fat 10.7 g
- Carbohydrates 6.7 g
- Sugar 5.2 g
- Protein 52 g
- Cholesterol 152 mg

24-Smoked Soy Garlic Beef Jerky

Total Time: 1 hour 40 minutes

Serves: 6

Ingredients:
- 1 1/2 lbs lean beef, slice into 1/4 inch slices
- 3/4 Tsp garlic powder
- 1/4 cup Worcestershire sauce
- 3/4 cup light soy
- 1/2 cup brown sugar
- 3/4 Tsp salt

Directions:
- Add all ingredients into the zip lock bag and mix well and place in refrigerator for overnight.
- Preheat the smoker to 170 F/76 C.
- Drain meat well and place in smoker and smoke for 1 1/2 hours.
- Serve and enjoy.

Nutritional Value (Amount per Serving):
- Calories 290
- Fat 7.1 g
- Carbohydrates 18.5 g
- Sugar 13.8 g
- Protein 35.7 g
- Cholesterol 101 mg

25-BBQ thyme Smoked Brisket

Total Time: 5 hours 15 minutes

Serves: 8

Ingredients:
- 5 lbs beef brisket
- 1/2 cup ketchup
- 3 tbsp brown sugar
- 2 tbsp Dijon mustard
- 1 1/2 tbsp liquid smoke
- 14 oz beer
- 1/2 cup apple cider vinegar
- 2 tbsp canola oil
- 1 tbsp fresh chive, chopped
- 1 tsp dried thyme
- For the mustard base:
- 3 bay leaves, crushed
- 1 tbsp basil
- 3 tbsp chive, chopped

- 8 garlic cloves, minced
- 1/2 cup yellow mustard
- 1/2 cup Dijon mustard
- For rub:
- 3 tbsp brown sugar
- 3 tbsp chili powder
- 1 tbsp rosemary
- 2 1/2 tbsp cumin powder
- 1 1/2 tbsp dry mustard
- 1 1/22 tbsp lemon zest
- 3 tbsp steak seasoning

Directions:

- Combine together all rub ingredients and rub all over brisket.
- Place brisket in a large zip lock bag and place in refrigerator for overnight.
- Remove brisket from refrigerator and set aside for 15 minutes.
- Now combine together all mustard base ingredients and brush over the brisket.
- Preheat the smoker at 225 F/107 C using wood chips.
- Place brisket in smoker and smoke for 3 hours.
- Meanwhile, for the marinade in an aluminum pan combine together ketchup, brown sugar, Dijon mustard, liquid smoke, beer, vinegar, canola oil, chive, and thyme.
- After 3 hours place brisket in aluminum pan and place in smoker.
- Cook continues for 2 hours and every half hour brush marinade over brisket.
- Cut into the slices and serve.

Nutritional Value (Amount per Serving):

- Calories 647
- Fat 23 g
- Carbohydrates 14.2 g
- Sugar 7.3 g
- Protein 88.1 g
- Cholesterol 253 mg

26-Smoke Corned Beef

Total Time: 6 hours 10 minutes

Serves: 8

Ingredients:
- 5 lbs corned beef, ready to cook
- 2 tbsp yellow mustard seeds
- 1/4 cup whole coriander seeds
- 1/4 cup whole black peppercorns

Directions:
- Rinse corned beef well and place in a large bowl.
- Pour water into the beef bowl and place bowl in refrigerator for at least 6 hours.
- Drain the meat and dry well with paper towel.
- Add spices in a grinder and crush until coarse.
- Coat meat with coarse spice mixture.

- Preheat the smoker to 225 F/107 C and place meat in smoker and smoke for 3 hours.
- Remove meat from smoker and place to pan.
- Add water in the bottom of the pan and cover the pan with foil.
- Bake in the oven at 250 F/121 C for 3 hours.
- Cut into the slices and serve.

Nutritional Value (Amount per Serving):

- Calories 497
- Fat 36.3 g
- Carbohydrates 1.8 g
- Sugar 0.2 g
- Protein 38.8 g
- Cholesterol 177 mg

27-Smoked Beef Patties

Total Time: 40 minutes

Serves: 10

Ingredients:
- 2 lbs ground beef
- 1 lb ground sausage
- 1 tsp hot paprika
- 1 tsp garlic powder
- 1 tsp black pepper
- 1 tsp sea salt

Directions:
- Add all ingredients into the mixing bowl and mix well.
- Make small round shape patties from mixture and place in smoker.
- Smoke patties at 200 F/93 C for 30 minutes.
- Serve and enjoy.

Nutritional Value (Amount per Serving):

- Calories 324
- Fat 18.5 g
- Carbohydrates 0.3 g
- Sugar 0.1 g
- Protein 36.4 g
- Cholesterol 119 mg

28-Smoked Meatloaf

Total Time: 4 hours 15 minutes

Serves: 6

Ingredients:
- For loaf:
- 2 lbs ground beef
- 6 oz pepper jack cheese, cut into strips
- 1/4 cup milk
- 1 tbsp steak rub
- 1 tbsp Worcestershire sauce
- 2 eggs, beaten
- 1 garlic cloves, minced
- 1/2 onion, grated
- 1/2 cup breadcrumbs
- For sauce:
- 2 tsp red pepper flakes, crushed

- 1 tbsp steak rub
- 1/3 cup brown sugar
- 1/2 cup ketchup

Directions:

- Preheat the smoker to 225 F/107 C using oak wood.
- In a large bowl, combine together all loaf ingredients.
- Spread half meatloaf mixture on grill basket then top with cheese.
- Now spread remaining meatloaf mixture over the cheese and press the edges well.
- In a small bowl, combine together all sauce ingredients and pour over meatloaf.
- Place meatloaf in the smoker and smoke for 4 hours or until internal temperature reaches 165 F.
- Cut meatloaf into the slices and serve.

Nutritional Value (Amount per Serving):

- Calories 521
- Fat 21.1 g
- Carbohydrates 23 g
- Sugar 14.5 g
- Protein 57 g
- Cholesterol 221 mg

29-Meat Wrapped Jalapeno Peppers

Total Time: 2 hours 10 minutes

Serves: 5

Ingredients:
- 1 lb ground beef
- 3/4 cup cheddar cheese, grated
- 4 oz cream cheese
- 5 jalapeno peppers, core and remove seeds
- Pepper
- Salt

Directions:
- Preheat the smoker to 250 F/121 C using pecan wood.
- Combine together cream cheese and grated cheddar cheese.
- Stuff cheese mixture into the jalapeno peppers.
- Season ground beef with pepper and salt.
- Wrap ground beef around the jalapeno peppers.
- Place wrapped jalapeno peppers on the smoker rack and smoke for 2 hours.

- Serve and enjoy.

Nutritional Value (Amount per Serving):
- Calories 322
- Fat 19.4 g
- Carbohydrates 1.9 g
- Sugar 0.6 g
- Protein 33.7 g
- Cholesterol 124 mg

30-Smoked Meatballs

Total Time: 1 hour 15 minutes

Serves: 20

Ingredients:
- 1 lb ground beef
- 1 lb ground pork
- 1/2 cup BBQ sauce
- 1 tsp red pepper flakes
- 12 oz smoked bacon, chopped
- 4 garlic cloves, minced
- 1/4 cup fresh parsley, chopped
- 1/2 cup Romano cheese, grated
- 1/3 cup milk
- 1/2 cup breadcrumbs

Directions:

- In a large bowl, soak breadcrumbs in milk for 5 minutes.
- Add remaining ingredients except for BBQ sauce into the bowl and mix well.
- Make small round shape meatballs from the mixture.
- Preheat the smoker to 300 F/148 F using apple wood.
- Place meatballs into the smoker and smoke for 30 minutes.
- After 30 minutes brush BBQ sauce over the meatballs and smoker for 15 minutes.
- Once 15 minutes is over then brush again meatballs with BBQ sauce and smoke for another 15 minutes.
- Serve and enjoy.

Nutritional Value (Amount per Serving):

- Calories 200
- Fat 10.4 g
- Carbohydrates 5 g
- Sugar 2 g
- Protein 20.5 g
- Cholesterol 58 mg

POULTRY RECIPES

31-Smoke Whole Chicken

Total Time: 4 hours 10 minutes

Serves: 4

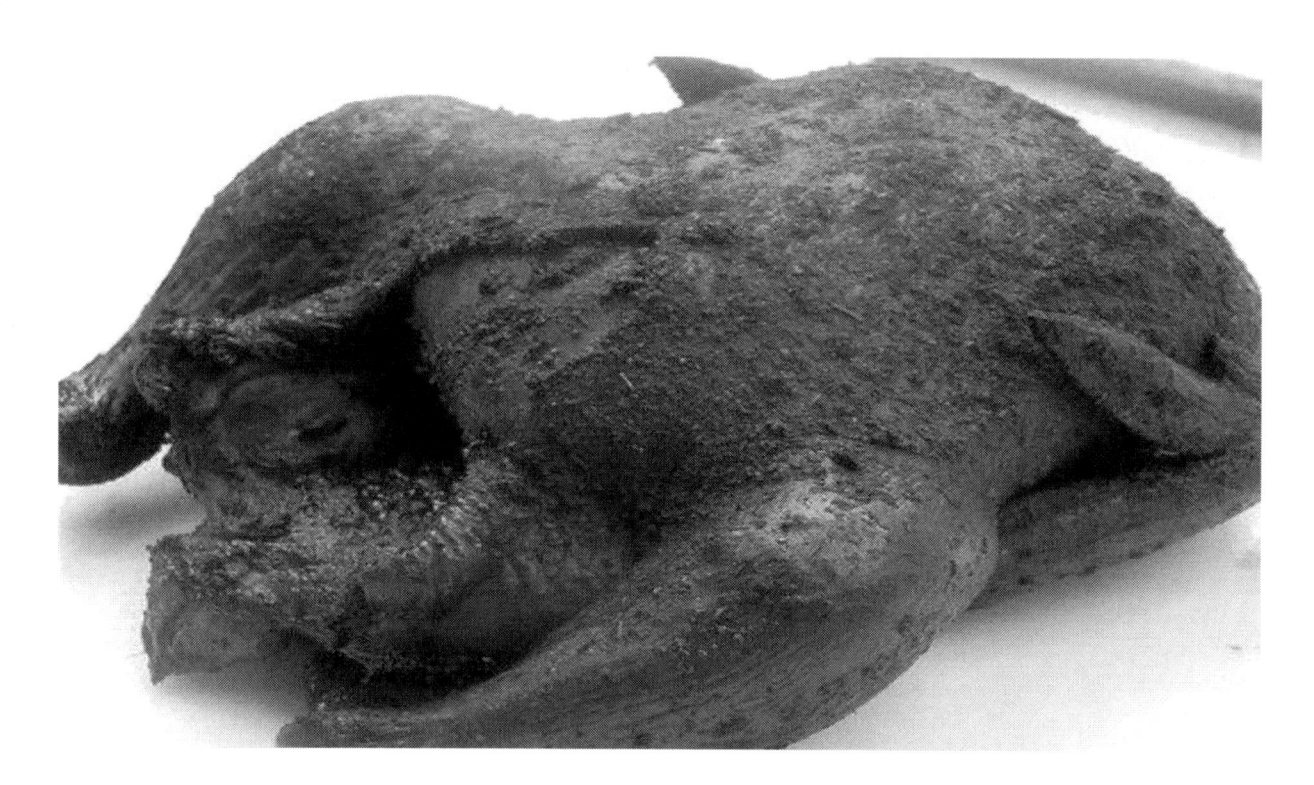

Ingredients:
- 2 lbs whole chicken, rinse and trim
- 3 tbsp dry rub

Directions:
- Preheat the smoker to 250 F/121 C using oak wood.
- Tie chicken legs together using kitchen string.
- Coat chicken well with dry rub.
- Place chicken in smoker and smoke until internal temperature reaches 165 F/73 C about 3-4 hours.
- Cut into the slices and serve.

Nutritional Value (Amount per Serving):

- Calories 442
- Fat 16.8 g
- Carbohydrates 2.3 g
- Sugar 0 g
- Protein 65.6 g
- Cholesterol 202 mg

32-Smoky Wrap Chicken Breasts

Total Time: 5 hours 30 minutes

Serves: 6

Ingredients:
- 6 chicken breasts, skinless and boneless
- 18 bacon slices
- 3 tbsp chicken rub
- For brine:
- 1/4 cup brown sugar
- 1/4 cup kosher salt
- 4 cups water

Directions:
- Combine together all brine ingredients into the glass dish.
- Place chicken into the dish and coat well.
- Soak chicken about 2 hours.

- Rinse chicken well and coat with chicken rub.
- Wrap each chicken breast with three bacon slices.
- Preheat the smoker to 230 F/110 C using soaked wood chips.
- Place wrapped chicken breasts into the smoker and smoke for about 3 hours or until internal temperature reaches 165 F/73 C.
- Serve and enjoy.

Nutritional Value (Amount per Serving):

- Calories 454
- Fat 14.4 g
- Carbohydrates 8.9 g
- Sugar 8.9 g
- Protein 32.8 g
- Cholesterol 101 mg

33-Smoked Chipotle Chicken Wings

Total Time: 2 hours 40 minutes

Serves: 6

Ingredients:

- 5 1/2 lbs chicken wings
- 1/2 tbsp ground cumin
- 1 tbsp ground mustard
- 1 tbsp smoked paprika
- 1 1/2 tbsp chipotle ground pepper
- 2 tbsp brown sugar
- 1/2 tbsp salt

Directions:

- Add all ingredients into the large zip lock bag and mix well and place the bag into the refrigerator for 30 minutes.
- Preheat the smoker to 250 F/121 C using wood chips.

- Remove chicken from refrigerator and place in smoker and smoke for 2 hours.
- Serve hot and enjoy.

Nutritional Value (Amount per Serving):

- Calories 815
- Fat 31.6 g
- Carbohydrates 4.5 g
- Sugar 3.2 g
- Protein 121 g
- Cholesterol 370 mg

34-Delicious Smoked Pulled Chicken

Total Time: 4 hours 10 minutes

Serves: 6

Ingredients:

- 3 lbs chicken
- 1/2 cup BBQ rub
- 1/2 cup butter

Directions:

- In a bowl, combine together butter and 2 tbsp BBQ rub.
- Rub butter mixture all over the chicken.
- Sprinkle remaining BBQ rub over the chicken.
- Using foil wrap the chicken well.
- Preheat the smoker to 230 F/110 F using wood chips.
- Place chicken in smoker and smoker for 3 1/2 hours or until internal temperature reaches 165 F/73 C.

- Unwrap the chicken and smoke for another 30 minutes.
- Using fork shred the chicken and serves.

Nutritional Value (Amount per Serving):

- Calories 478
- Fat 22.2 g
- Carbohydrates 0 g
- Sugar 0 g
- Protein 65.9 g
- Cholesterol 215 mg

35-Smoked Chicken Thighs

Total Time: 4 hours 10 minutes

Serves: 6

Ingredients:
- 24 oz chicken thighs, skin on
- 2 tbsp black pepper
- 2 tbsp cayenne
- 1 tbsp garlic powder
- 1 tbsp thyme
- 2 tbsp chili powder
- 2 tbsp paprika
- 1 cup olive oil
- 1 tbsp salt

Directions:
- Preheat the smoker to 200 F/93 C using wood chips.
- Combine all dry seasoning ingredients together.

- Coat chicken with olive oil then sprinkles seasoning over the chicken.
- Place chicken in smoker and smoke for 2 hours.
- After 2 hours flip the chicken and smoker for another 2 hours or until internal temperature reaches 165 F/73 C.
- Serve and enjoy.

Nutritional Value (Amount per Serving):

- Calories 535
- Fat 43.1 g
- Carbohydrates 6.3 g
- Sugar 1 g
- Protein 34.2 g
- Cholesterol 101 mg

36-Simple Turkey Breast

Total Time: 5 hours 5 minutes

Serves: 8

Ingredients:
- 5 lbs turkey breast
- 1/2 cup chicken rub seasoning

Directions:
- Preheat the smoker to 225 F/107 C using wood chips.
- Wash turkey and pat dry using a paper towel.
- Rub chicken seasoning over the turkey and place in smoker.
- Smoke turkey about 5 hours or until internal temperature reaches 165 F/73 C.
- Serve and enjoy.

Nutritional Value (Amount per Serving):
- Calories 310

- Fat 5 g
- Carbohydrates 14.9 g
- Sugar 11 g
- Protein 48.9 g
- Cholesterol 122 mg

37-Tasty Smoked Chicken Tenders

Total Time: 1 hour 10 minutes

Serves: 8

Ingredients:

- 4 lbs chicken tenders, rinsed and pat dry
- 1/4 Tsp Cajun seasoning
- 3/4 Tsp fresh ginger, grated
- 2 tsp garlic, minced
- 1 1/2 tbsp sesame seeds
- 1/4 cup water
- 1/2 cup olive oil
- 1/2 cup soy sauce

Directions:

- Add all ingredients into the zip lock bag and mix well and place in refrigerator for overnight.
- Preheat the smoker to 225 F/107 C using wood chips.

- Remove chicken tenders from marinade and place on middle rack of smoker and smoke for 1 hour or until internal temperature reaches 165 F/73 C.
- Serve and enjoy.

Nutritional Value (Amount per Serving):

- Calories 559
- Fat 30.3 g
- Carbohydrates 2 g
- Sugar 0.3 g
- Protein 67 g
- Cholesterol 202 mg

38-Cajun Seasoned Chicken Breast

Total Time: 4 hours 10 minutes

Serves: 4

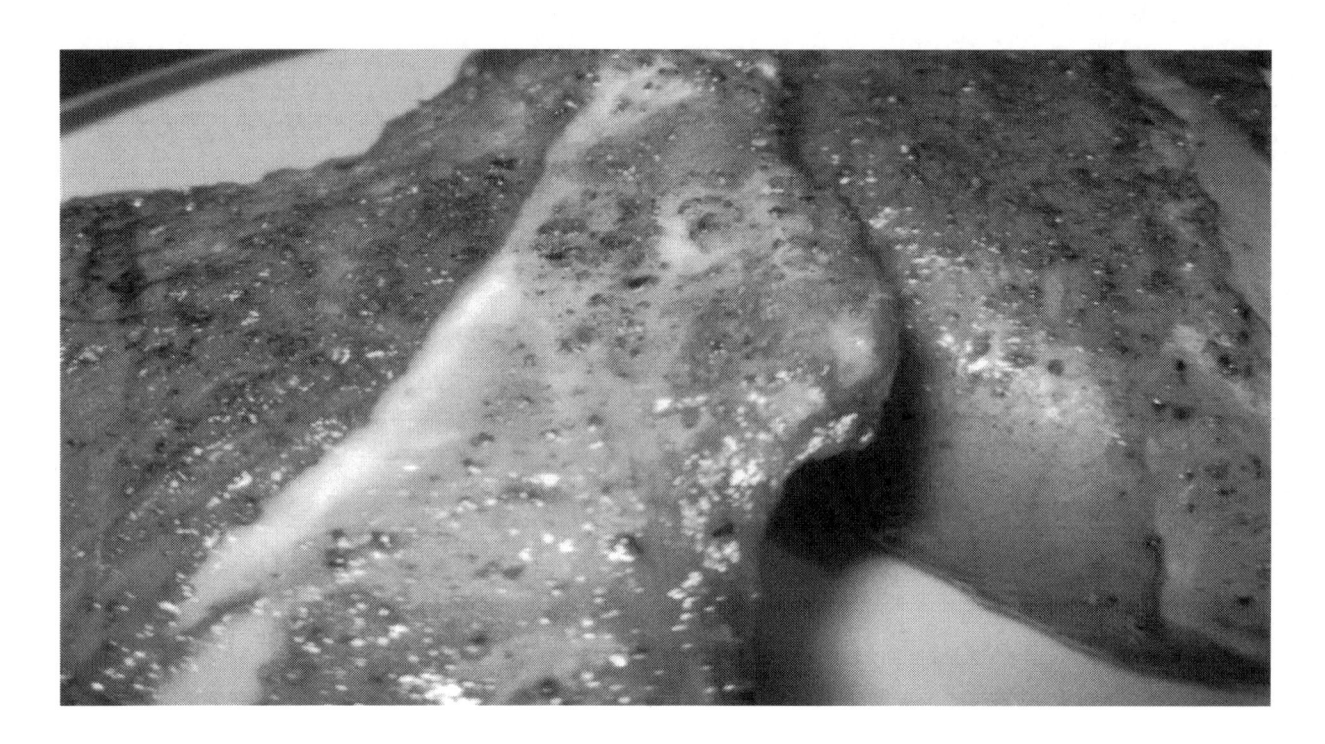

Ingredients:

- 2 lbs chicken breasts, boneless
- 1 cup BBQ sauce
- 2 tbsp Cajun seasoning

Directions:

- Preheat the smoker to 225 F/107 C using apple wood chips.
- Rub chicken with Cajun seasoning and place on the smoker rack and smoke for 4 hours or until internal temperature reaches 165 F/73 C.
- Coat chicken with BBQ sauce during the last hour of cooking.
- Serve and enjoy.

Nutritional Value (Amount per Serving):

- Calories 525

- Fat 17 g
- Carbohydrates 22.7 g
- Sugar 16.3 g
- Protein 65.7 g
- Cholesterol 202 mg

39-Orange Smoked Chicken

Total Time: 2 hours 10 minutes

Serves: 3

Ingredients:

- 12 oz chicken breasts, rinse and trim excess fat
- For rub:
- 2 tbsp chicken rub seasoning
- For marinade:
- 1 tbsp garlic powder
- 1/2 cup soy sauce
- 2 cups orange juice

Directions:

- Add chicken and marinade ingredients into the zip lock bag and mix well.
- Place chicken bag in the refrigerator for overnight.
- Preheat the smoker to 250 F/121 C using apple wood chips.

- Remove chicken from marinade and rub chicken seasoning over the chicken.
- Place chicken in smoker and smoker for 2 hours or until internal temperature reaches 165 F/73 C.
- Serve and enjoy.

Nutritional Value (Amount per Serving):

- Calories 322
- Fat 8.8 g
- Carbohydrates 22.5 g
- Sugar 15.3 g
- Protein 37.1 g
- Cholesterol 101 mg

40-Smoked Soy Chicken Legs

Total Time: 4 hours 10 minutes

Serves: 4

Ingredients:

- 3 1/2 lbs chicken legs, rinse and pat dry
- 2 cups apple juice
- 1/4 cup BBQ spice
- 1/2 cup soy sauce
- 1/2 cup Italian salad dressing

Directions:

- Add chicken, BBQ spice, soy sauce, and Italian salad dressing in zip lock bag and mix well.
- Place chicken bag in the refrigerator for overnight.
- Preheat the smoker to 250 F/121 C using apple wood.
- Remove chicken from marinade and place in smoker and smoke for 4 hours.
- After every 30 minutes misting with apple juice.

- Serve and enjoy.

Nutritional Value (Amount per Serving):

- Calories 928
- Fat 37.9 g
- Carbohydrates 23 g
- Sugar 18.5 g
- Protein 117 g
- Cholesterol 373 mg

41-Delicious Honey Smoked Chicken

Total Time: 2 hours 10 minutes

Serves: 4

Ingredients:

- 16 oz chicken breasts, skinless and boneless
- For seasoning:
- 1 tsp onion powder
- 1 tsp garlic powder
- 1 tsp Chinese five spice
- For marinade:
- 2 tbsp soy sauce
- 1/4 cup honey
- 3/4 cup orange juice

Directions:

- Add all marinade ingredients into the microwave safe bowl and microwave for 30 seconds.
- Add chicken and marinade into the zip lock bag and mix well.
- Place marinated chicken in refrigerator for 1 hour.
- Combine together all seasoning ingredients and set aside.
- Preheat the smoker to 250 F/121 C using apple wood.
- Remove chicken from marinade and sprinkle with seasoning mixture from both the sides.
- Place chicken in smoker and smoke for 30 minutes then flip chicken and smoke for another 20 minutes or until internal temperature reaches 155 F/68 C.
- Serve and enjoy.

Nutritional Value (Amount per Serving):

- Calories 310
- Fat 8.5 g
- Carbohydrates 23.9 g
- Sugar 21.8 g
- Protein 33.9 g
- Cholesterol 101 mg

42-Smoked Buffalo Chicken Wings

Total Time: 4 hours 40 minutes

Serves: 8

Ingredients:

- 5 lbs chicken wings, rinse and pat dry
- Pepper
- Salt
- For sauce:
- 2 tbsp butter
- 1 cup red hot sauce

Directions:

- Place chicken wings into the refrigerator for 3 hours.
- Preheat the smoker to 225 F/107 C.
- Remove chicken wings from refrigerator and coat with little olive oil.
- Season chicken wings with pepper and salt.

- Place chicken wings in the smoker for 1 hour.
- After 1-hour increase temperature to 350 F/176 C and smoke for another 30 minutes.
- In a bowl, combine together sauce ingredients.
- Add smoked chicken wings into the bowl and toss well.
- Serve and enjoy.

Nutritional Value (Amount per Serving):

- Calories 567
- Fat 24 g
- Carbohydrates 0.5 g
- Sugar 0.4 g
- Protein 82.2 g
- Cholesterol 260 mg

43-Moist Wrapped Chicken Tenders

Total Time: 40 minutes

Serves: 5

Ingredients:
- 1 lb chicken tenders
- 1 tbsp chili powder
- 1/3 cup brown sugar
- 1 tsp garlic powder
- 1 tsp onion powder
- 1 tsp paprika
- 1/2 Tsp Italian seasoning
- 10 bacon slices
- 1/2 Tsp pepper
- 1/2 Tsp salt

Directions:

- Preheat the smoker to 350 F/176 C.
- In a bowl, combine together Italian seasoning, garlic powder, onion powder, paprika, pepper, and salt.
- Add chicken tenders to the bowl and toss well.
- Wrap each chicken tenders with a bacon slice.
- Mix together chili powder and brown sugar and sprinkle over the wrapped chicken.
- Place wrapped the chicken in smoker and smoke for 30 minutes.
- Serve and enjoy.

Nutritional Value (Amount per Serving):

- Calories 247
- Fat 7.9 g
- Carbohydrates 11.5 g
- Sugar 9.9 g
- Protein 26.7 g
- Cholesterol 81 mg

44-Sweet and Spicy Chicken Wings

Total Time: 1 hour 20 minutes

Serves: 8

Ingredients:

- 5 lbs chicken wings, rinsed and pat dry
- 3 tbsp apple juice
- 1/2 cup BBQ sauce
- 1 cup honey
- 1 tbsp garlic powder
- 1 tbsp chili powder
- 1 tbsp onion powder
- 2 1/2 tbsp ground black pepper
- 1 tbsp seasoned salt

Directions:

- Combine together black pepper, seasoned salt, garlic powder, chili powder, and onion powder.
- Add chicken wings into the zip lock bag then pour dry rub mixture over the chicken and mix well.
- Place chicken bag into the refrigerator for overnight.
- Preheat the smoker to 225 F/107 C using apple wood chips.
- Place chicken wings in smoker and smoke for 20 minutes.
- After 20 minutes turn chicken and smoke for another 25 minutes or until internal temperature reach 165 F/73 C.
- Meanwhile, in a small saucepan combine together BBQ sauce, honey, and apple juice and cook over medium heat.
- Remove chicken wings from smoker and toss with BBQ sauce mixture.
- Return chicken wings into the smoker and smoke for another 25 minutes.
- Serve hot and enjoy.

Nutritional Value (Amount per Serving):

- Calories 748
- Fat 21.4 g
- Carbohydrates 54.4 g
- Sugar 48.5 g
- Protein 82.8 g
- Cholesterol 252 mg

45-Simple Smoked Chicken Wings

Total Time: 1 hour 10 minutes

Serves: 8

Ingredients:

- 4 lbs chicken wings
- 1 bottle Italian dressing
- 3 tbsp chicken rub seasoning

Directions:

- Add Italian dressing and chicken wings into the zip lock bag and place in refrigerator for overnight.
- Drain chicken well and rub chicken seasoning over chicken wings.
- Preheat the smoker to 300 F/148 C using apple wood.
- Place coated chicken wings in the smoker and smoke for 1 hour.
- Serve hot and enjoy.

Nutritional Value (Amount per Serving):

- Calories 431
- Fat 16.8 g
- Carbohydrates 0 g
- Sugar 0 g
- Protein 65.6 g
- Cholesterol 202 mg

SEAFOOD RECIPES

46-Smoked Cajun Seasoned Shrimp

Total Time: 40 minutes

Serves: 4

Ingredients:
- 1 lb fresh shrimp, peeled and deveined
- 3 tbsp hot sauce
- 1/3 cup ranch salad dressing
- 1/2 Tsp cayenne pepper
- 1/2 Tsp ground black pepper
- 1/2 Tsp thyme
- 1 tsp oregano
- 1 tsp onion powder
- 1 tsp garlic powder
- 1 1/2 Tsp paprika

- 2 tbsp olive oil
- 1 1/2 Tsp salt

Directions:

- In a large bowl, toss shrimp with cayenne pepper, black pepper, thyme, oregano, onion powder, garlic powder, paprika, oil, and salt.
- Preheat the smoker to 225 F/107 C using apple wood.
- Place shrimp in smoker and smoke for 30 minutes or until shrimp turn pink.
- Meanwhile, for dip whisk together hot sauce and ranch salad dressing.
- Serve shrimp with prepared dip and enjoy.

Nutritional Value (Amount per Serving):

- Calories 212
- Fat 9.2 g
- Carbohydrates 5.1 g
- Sugar 1.2 g
- Protein 26.6 g
- Cholesterol 239 mg

47-Simple Smoke Trout

Total Time: 1 hour 10 minutes

Serves: 2

Ingredients:
- 2 medium trout, cleaned
- 1 tsp butter
- 1 medium onion, sliced
- 1/2 cup salad dressing

Directions:
- Add salad dressing and trout in zip lock bag and place in refrigerator for overnight.
- Preheat the smoker to 150 F/65 C using pecan wood.
- Place 1/2 Tsp butter and onion into the fish cavity then place trout in the smoker.

- Smoke trout for 30 minutes. After 30 minutes increase temperature to 225 F/107 C and smoke for 30 minutes.
- Serve and enjoy.

Nutritional Value (Amount per Serving):

- Calories 388
- Fat 26.7 g
- Carbohydrates 19.2 g
- Sugar 6.1 g
- Protein 18.4 g
- Cholesterol 69 mg

48-Smoked Fish Nuggets

Total Time: 4 hours 10 minutes

Serves: 4

Ingredients:
- 4 lbs fresh salmon fillets
- 1 tsp ground cayenne
- 1 tbsp ground black pepper
- 2 tbsp onion powder
- 2 tbsp garlic powder
- 6 cups brown sugar
- 2 cups coarse kosher salt

Directions:
- Cut the salmon skin and wash fish.
- Pat dry salmon with a paper towel and cut into 1" cubes.

- In a bowl, combine together all remaining ingredients add salmon in a bowl and toss well and place in refrigerator for 6 hours.
- Remove salmon from refrigerator and wash well using cold water.
- Place salmon cubes on a flat surface and allow drying.
- Preheat the smoker to 120 F/48 C using pecan wood.
- Place salmon cubes in smoker and smoke for 4 hours.
- Serve and enjoy.

Nutritional Value (Amount per Serving):

- Calories 630
- Fat 28.1 g
- Carbohydrates 6.9 g
- Sugar 2.3 g
- Protein 89.2 g
- Cholesterol 200 mg

49-Smoked Orange Sesame Salmon

Total Time: 3 hours 10 minutes

Serves: 4

Ingredients:
- 2 lbs salmon fillet
- 1 tbsp sesame seeds, toasted
- 1 tsp garlic powder
- 2 tbsp sesame oil
- 1 1/2 tbsp sriracha sauce
- 1/2 cup honey
- 2/3 cup orange juice
- 1/2 cup hoisin sauce

Directions:
- In a small bowl, for marinade combine together garlic powder, sesame oil, sriracha sauce, honey, orange juice, and hoisin sauce.

- Place salmon fillet in a flat dish.
- Pour half marinade over the fish fillet and cover and place in refrigerator for 3 hours.
- Preheat the smoker to 250 F/121 C using apple wood chips.
- Place marinated fish in smoker and smoke for 3 hours or until internal temperature reaches 145 F/62 C.
- Meanwhile, for glaze: add remaining marinade in small saucepan and heat over medium heat for 10 minutes or until thickened.
- Place salmon on serving dish and brush with glaze and sprinkle with sesame seeds.
- Serve and enjoy.

Nutritional Value (Amount per Serving):

- Calories 631
- Fat 26.8 g
- Carbohydrates 54.8 g
- Sugar 47.6 g
- Protein 46 g
- Cholesterol 105 mg

50-Smoked Wrapped Scallops

Total Time: 2 hours 30 minutes

Serves: 6

Ingredients:

- 12 sea scallops
- 1 lb bacon slices
- 2 tbsp Jeff's rub
- 2 tbsp olive oil

Directions:

- Add scallops, rub, and olive oil in zip lock bag and mix well.
- Place bag in the refrigerator for 1 hour.
- Remove scallops from the refrigerator and wrap in bacon slices.
- Sprinkle remaining rub over bacon wrapped scallops.
- Place wrapped scallops in smoker and smoke for 1 hour or until internal temperature reaches 145 F/62 C.

- Serve hot and enjoy.

Nutritional Value (Amount per Serving):

- Calories 471
- Fat 37.5 g
- Carbohydrates 1.4 g
- Sugar 0 g
- Protein 31.7 g
- Cholesterol 101 mg

51-Easy Smoked Tuna

Total Time: 7 hours 10 minutes

Serves: 4

Ingredients:
- 4 tuna steaks
- 1-gallon water
- 1 cup honey
- 1/4 Tsp garlic, minced
- 1 tsp pepper
- 1 1/8 cup sugar

Directions:
- Add all ingredients except tuna into the pan and mix well.
- Place tuna into the pan.
- Preheat the smoker to 140 F/60 C using apple wood.
- Place tuna pan in the smoker and cook for 7 hours.

- Serve and enjoy.

Nutritional Value (Amount per Serving):

- Calories 650
- Fat 1.5 g
- Carbohydrates 126.5 g
- Sugar 125.9 g
- Protein 40.3 g
- Cholesterol 75 mg

52-Delicious Smoked Shrimp

Total Time: 55 minutes

Serves: 6

Ingredients:
- 3 lbs shrimp
- 1 tsp nutmeg
- 1 tsp paprika
- 1 tsp cumin
- 1 tbsp oregano
- 1 tbsp sweet basil
- 1/8 cup cayenne pepper
- 1/8 cup black pepper, crushed
- 1/4 cup hot sauce
- 1/3 cup Worcestershire sauce
- 1 1/2 sticks butter

Directions:

- Melt butter in a pan over medium heat.
- Remove pan from heat and add hot sauce and Worcestershire sauce in butter pan and mix well.
- Add shrimp in a pan and mix well.
- Combine together all dry ingredients and pour over the shrimp. Toss well.
- Preheat the smoker to 230 F/110 C using apple wood.
- Place shrimp in smoker and smoke for 45 minutes.
- Serve and enjoy.

Nutritional Value (Amount per Serving):

- Calories 501
- Fat 27.5 g
- Carbohydrates 8.9 g
- Sugar 3.2 g
- Protein 52.5 g
- Cholesterol 538 mg

53-Smoked Dill Salmon

Total Time: 2 hours 10 minutes

Serves: 6

Ingredients:
- 2 lbs salmon
- 2 tbsp brown sugar
- 1 tsp dill
- 1 tsp black pepper
- 1 tsp salt

Directions:
- Preheat the smoker to 250 F/121 C using pecan wood.
- Combine together brown sugar, dill, pepper, and salt.
- Pat gently brown sugar mixture over salmon and place in refrigerator for 1 hour.

- Place salmon in smoker and smoke for 1 hour or until internal temperature reaches 145 F/62 C.
- Serve and enjoy.

Nutritional Value (Amount per Serving):

- Calories 213
- Fat 9.4 g
- Carbohydrates 3.3 g
- Sugar 2.9 g
- Protein 29.4 g
- Cholesterol 67 mg

54-Easy BBQ Shrimp

Total Time: 1 hour 5 minutes

Serves: 10

Ingredients:
- 40 fresh shrimp, peeled and deveined
- 18 oz BBQ sauce
- 5 wooden skewers, soaked in water for 30 minutes

Directions:
- Preheat the smoker to 235 F/112 C using hickory wood.
- Thread shrimp on soaked skewers and place in smoker and smoke for 40 minutes.
- When shrimp is cooked then brush with BBQ sauce and cook for another 5 minutes.
- Serve and enjoy.

Nutritional Value (Amount per Serving):

- Calories 181
- Fat 1.6 g
- Carbohydrates 19.8 g
- Sugar 13.3 g
- Protein 20 g
- Cholesterol 185 mg

55-Maple Peppercorns Smoked Salmon

Total Time: 2 hours 5 minutes

Serves: 4

Ingredients:
- 1 lb fresh salmon fillet
- 1/2 cup maple syrup
- 1 tbsp peppercorns, crushed
- 2 tbsp water
- 2 tbsp pure maple syrup
- 1/4 Tsp salt

Directions:
- Rinse salmon and pat dry with paper towel.
- Add salmon, 1/2 cup maple syrup, peppercorns, water, and salt in large zip lock bag and mix well.
- Place salmon bag in the refrigerator for 1 hour.

- Preheat the smoker to 225 F/107 C using apple wood.
- Pour water into the pan.
- Place salmon in smoker skin side down and on grill rack over the water pan.
- Cover salmon and smoke for 50 minutes.
- Brush salmon with maple syrup.
- Serve hot and enjoy.

Nutritional Value (Amount per Serving):

- Calories 269
- Fat 7.1 g
- Carbohydrates 30.8 g
- Sugar 26.8 g
- Protein 22.2 g
- Cholesterol 50 mg

56-Simple Smoked Lobster Tails

Total Time: 40 minutes

Serves: 4

Ingredients:

- 4 lobster tails
- 4 garlic cloves, minced
- 1/4 cup butter, melted

Directions:

- Preheat the smoker to 400 F/204 C using pecan wood chips.
- Open lobster tails using a kitchen knife.
- Combine together butter and garlic and drizzle over lobster.
- Place lobster in smoker and smoke until internal temperature reaches 130 F/54 C.
- Serve and enjoy.

Nutritional Value (Amount per Serving):

- Calories 269
- Fat 7.1 g
- Carbohydrates 30.8 g
- Sugar 26.8 g
- Protein 22.2 g
- Cholesterol 50 mg

57-Smoked Lemon Dill Salmon

Total Time: 40 minutes

Serves: 4

Ingredients:

- 4 salmon fillets, with skin, wash and pat dry
- 1 onion, sliced
- 2 lemons, sliced
- 1/2 Tsp black pepper
- 1/2 Tsp fresh dill

Directions:

- Preheat the smoker to 220 F/104 C using apple wood chips.
- Place salmon fillet skin side down on baking sheet.
- In a small bowl, combine together black pepper and fresh dill.
- Sprinkle salmon fillet with dill pepper mixture.
- Place lemon and onion slices over the salmon.

- Place salmon on bottom rack of smoker and smoke for 30 minutes.
- Serve and enjoy.

Nutritional Value (Amount per Serving):

- Calories 256
- Fat 11.1 g
- Carbohydrates 5.5 g
- Sugar 1.9 g
- Protein 35.2 g
- Cholesterol 78 mg

58-Stuffed Salmon

Total Time: 3 hours 10 minutes

Serves: 8

Ingredients:
- 4 lbs salmon
- 1 garlic clove, minced
- 1/2 Tsp lemon pepper
- 1/4 cup celery, chopped
- 1/2 cup dry bread cubes
- 1/4 cup fresh dill, chopped
- 1 cup tomato, peeled and chopped
- 1/4 cup green onions, chopped
- 3 tbsp olive oil

Directions:
- Coat salmon with olive oil.

- Add all ingredients except salmon into the bowl and mix well.
- Stuff bowl mixture into the salmon.
- Place salmon on aluminum foil.
- Preheat the smoker to 225 F/107 C using pecan wood.
- Place salmon in smoker and smoke for 3 hours.
- Serve and enjoy.

Nutritional Value (Amount per Serving):

- Calories 355
- Fat 19.4 g
- Carbohydrates 2.3 g
- Sugar 0.7 g
- Protein 44.6 g
- Cholesterol 100 mg

59-Delicious Sweet Salmon

Total Time: 3 hours 15 minutes

Serves: 4

Ingredients:
- 3 lbs salmon fillets
- 1/2 cup white sugar
- 1/2 cup brown sugar
- 1 tsp black pepper
- 1/2 cup kosher salt
- For rub:
- 1 tbsp garlic powder
- 1/3 cup brown sugar
- 1/4 cup paprika

Directions:

- In a bowl, combine together white sugar, black pepper, brown sugar, and kosher salt.
- Add salmon and bowl mixture into the large zip lock bag and mix well and place in refrigerator for overnight.
- Remove salmon from refrigerator and rinse well and pat dry with paper towel.
- Combine together all rub ingredients and rub over salmon.
- Place salmon in smoker and smoke for 1-2 hours or until internal temperature reaches 150 F/65 C.
- Serve and enjoy.

Nutritional Value (Amount per Serving):

- Calories 521
- Fat 21.8 g
- Carbohydrates 16.9 g
- Sugar 12.9 g
- Protein 67.3 g
- Cholesterol 150 mg

60-Fresh and Simple Smoked Albacore Tuna

Total Time: 3 hours 10 minutes

Serves: 6

Ingredients:

- 6 albacore tuna fillets
- 1 orange zest
- 1 lemon zest
- 1 cup brown sugar
- 1 cup kosher salt

Directions:

- In a bowl, combine together orange zest, lemon zest, brown sugar, and kosher salt.
- Add bowl mixture and tuna fillets in large zip lock bag and mix well and place in refrigerator for 6 hours.
- Remove tuna fillets from brine and rinse well. Pat dry with paper towel.
- Preheat the smoker to 250 F/121 C using pecan wood.

- Place tuna fillets in the smoker and cook for 3 hours.
- Serve and enjoy.

Nutritional Value (Amount per Serving):
- Calories 170
  - Fat 3.6 g
  - Carbohydrates 6 g
  - Sugar 0 g
  - Protein 32.9 g
  - Cholesterol 50 mg

Made in the USA
Middletown, DE
20 November 2017